With My Very Best Wishes

Tin B Kikma

Order this book online at www.trafford.com/07-1792
or email orders@trafford.com

Most Trafford titles are also available at major online book retailers.

Note for Librarians: A cataloguing record for this book is available from Library and
Archives Canada at www.collectionscanada.ca/amicus/index-e.html
Printed in Victoria, BC, Canada.

Cover Artwork by Nichola J. Kirkman
Page Layout by Danielle Raine

ISBN: 978-1-4251-4294-0

*We at Trafford believe that it is the responsibility of us all, as both individuals and
corporations, to make choices that are environmentally and socially sound. You,
in turn, are supporting this responsible conduct each time you purchase a Trafford
book, or make use of our publishing services. To find out how you are helping,
please visit www.trafford.com/responsiblepublishing.html*

*Our mission is to efficiently provide the world's finest, most comprehensive book
publishing service, enabling every author to experience success. To find out how
to publish your book, your way, and have it available worldwide, visit us online at
www.trafford.com/10510*

www.trafford.com

North America & international

toll-free: 1888 232 4444 (USA & Canada)
phone: 250 383 6864 ♦ fax: 250 383 6804
email: info@trafford.com

The United Kingdom & Europe
phone: +44 (0)1865 722 113 ♦ local rate: 0845 230 9601
facsimile: +44 (0)1865 722 868 ♦ email:info.uk@trafford.com

10 9 8 7 6 5 4 3 2

**This edition printed and bound in Great Britain by
Printserve UK Ltd - October 2007
www.printserve.co.uk**

**Printed on Evolve Business 100% recycled paper
sourced from only post consumer waste.**

**Visit
www.my-guardian-angel-and-me.co.uk**

DEDICATED TO

MY FAMILY

ESPECIALLY

MY DAD,

WHO INSPIRED MY

LOVE OF WORDS

YOUR
GUARDIAN ANGEL
DAY BOOK

YOU WERE BORN WITH

A

GUARDIAN

ANGEL

...and
your name
on a
star.

YOU ARE UNIQUE

Only you can ever be you.

No-one else can carry out

the special tasks on earth

that you were

born to

accomplish.

LIFE'S
OPPORTUNITIES

Your

journey
through life
will cross paths

with people

who are destined to

change

your life

forever.

SMILE

WHENEVER YOU ARE HAPPY

...then everyone

who sees you smile

can share in your

happiness.

FACE UP TO LIFE'S CHALLENGES

You are

far braver

&

stronger

than you can

ever imagine.

THE POWER
OF
YOUR
INFLUENCE

Your influence
on others has the
potential
to
change
the world
&
the course of
history.

ANXIETY

...is the worry
or fear
of something
that may
never
happen.

HONESTY

Before you can

begin to show

honesty

to others

you have to be

honest

with

yourself.

HAVE

FAITH

Believe
in yourself
...and others will too.

THE WORLD
IS YOURS

Be bound
by what
unites
you
to the world
not
by what
divides
you from it.

HAVE A
POSITIVE
ATTITUDE

Thinking,
feeling
&
acting
positively

opens

new horizons

for aptitude

& achievement.

CAUTION:

ANGER

...is only

one letter away

from

DANGER.

YOU

ARE THE

GUARDIAN

OF

YOUR

DESTINY

...and
the steward
of all
that you
possess.

THE LIFE THAT IS YOURS

You
are the
guardian
of
how you live
&
the
choices
you make.

THE
PEOPLE
YOU MEET

...along

the

Path Of Life

are entrusted to your

care

&

influence.

MAKE TIME
FOR
YOURSELF

Take time

to be you

&

be proud

to be you.

HOLD ON
TO HOPE

When
all else
is
lost

hope is
always nearby.

WISDOM

...is knowing
when you are
right
&
when you are
wrong
&
acting
accordingly.

TRUE
INTEGRITY

...is being

honest

about yourself

to

yourself.

RESPONSIBILITY

You are the

Caretaker of your life,

your time,

your actions

&

the company you keep.

STRENGTH

Recognising
& accepting
your own
limitations
is
a great strength
& not
a weakness.

LOVE WHO YOU ARE

To

love others

you must

first

love

yourself.

ENDURANCE

You are
not beaten
unless
you give in,
give up
or
accept
defeat.

KINDNESS

Even the

smallest

act of kindness

will initiate

a ripple

that can travel

the

world.

ENCOURAGEMENT

...is

empowering

for what

is

right,

but it can

also be

empowering

to what is

wrong.

BE POSITIVE

If you think that you can -

you can.

It's when you think

that you can't -

that you won't.

PATIENCE

If you show patience

to those less able

than yourself

others will learn

to be patient

with them also.

DISAPPOINTMENTS

...are

opportunities
in disguise

to enable you to
reflect & reassess,

react &

learn to move on.

LIFE IS A

BALANCE

...of joy
& of pain,

of sun
& of rain,

of losses
& of gain.

LIVE EACH DAY

...as if it were your first.

Or your very last.

A

GUARDIAN

ANGEL

PRAYER

...is a wish
of love
with
hope
&
belief.

SPECIAL THANKS

DANIELLE,
NICHOLA,
MATTHEW
&
PAUL